A souvenir guide

The Courts Garden

Wiltshire

National Trust

A Hive of Industry

The garden at The Courts is a lyrical interpretation of an unpromising industrial site which has been transformed by successive owners throughout the 20th century into a relaxed and intensely personal garden.

An intimate garden

Few clues are given to what lies beyond the gate but as you enter, the garden is gradually revealed. The series of intimate garden rooms emphasise privacy and a separation from the outside world, a feature that defines many gardens during the early 20th century.

The mill was demolished at the end of the 19th century, leaving only the dwelling house (not open to the public) that now anchors the seven-acre garden. The ornate early Georgian

The Court, Hol¹, Wilts.

Above The house and mill around the end of the 19th century

Left The Courts, 1904

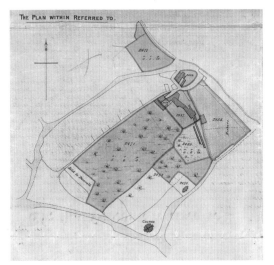
THE PLAN WITHIN REFERRED TO.

façade divides opinion. To Nicholas Pevsner in *Buildings of England* (1975) it is 'wildly overdone in all its details, an instructive example of what a vulgar mind can do with promising elements'. On the other hand Christopher Hussey writing for *Country Life* in 1943 admired the 'exquisite front elevation', and Timothy Mowl in *Historic Gardens of Wiltshire* (2004) is beguiled by its 'bucolic charm'. The idiosyncratic appeal of the house is carried through into the garden. Water plays a prominent role, the ponds and rills are reminiscent of the garden's previous industrial incarnation while hedges and topiary add structure and theatricality.

Out of the ashes

What you see today is the 20th-century transformation of this once industrial site into a very individual garden. The Arts and Crafts style of hedging and topiary is united with Italianate terraces and faux Georgian architectural elements. Garden axes are gently off kilter with the lines of the house and the dry-stone walling was roughly built. The garden is evidently the result of amateur creativity rather than a professional hand, enhancing the unashamedly domestic and

personal nature of the garden which has been allowed to evolve organically without the constraints of rigid plans.

The framework of the garden has changed little since it was laid out in the early 1900s by George Hastings, undaunted by the challenge of an unpromising wet site and hampered by industrial foundations. Since Major Clarence Goff gave The Courts to the National Trust in 1944, the spirit of the planting style, implemented in the 1920s and 30s by Lady Cecilie Goff with head gardener Rupert Stacey, has been continued and developed. Moyra Goff, Lady Cecilie's daughter, remained at The Courts until her death in 1990. Her main contribution was the development of the Arboretum which, at close to four acres comprises over half of the garden.

Left Holt Mills – the house, land and mill buildings shown on the conveyance plan of 1875 when John Davis sold the estate to Joseph Jones

Below The Rill today, a reminder of the garden's previous industrial history

From Factory to Family Home

The origin of the name 'The Courts' is unclear. One theory is that it refers to a manorial law court in Holt in 1545 that was held by Anthony Rogers. Later deeds refer to part of Henry Halliday's land as a 'court'; he was the owner of the property between 1769 and 1797.

There is also scant documentation about the early history of the house; parts of the present building are believed to date from the 16th and 17th centuries when it belonged to the Chapman, then the Showering families. The site's incarnation as a woollen mill (Holt Mills) from the early 18th century is better recorded.

Right The Courts, 1943

Below Map of garden with old mill buildings superimposed

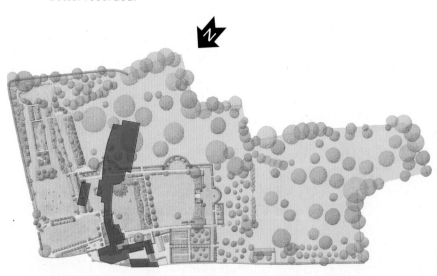

The mill – mixed fortunes

Holt, situated within the triangle of Wiltshire's most prosperous woollen textile centres of Bradford-on-Avon, Trowbridge and Melksham, was an ideal location for John Phelps, a Bradford-on-Avon cloth producer, to build spinning and weaving workshops. Having purchased The Courts' lease in 1703, Phelps added a new wing, and in around 1731 remodelled the earlier medieval house with a Georgian façade that welcomes the visitor today. When John Phelps died in 1734 the property, consisting of the house, garden, orchard, stable and land, together with the clothing houses, outhouses, dyehouses, dye furnaces, utensils and appurtenances, was left to his sons.

From water to steam

The house was to change hands several times until 1797 when it was bought by clothier John Davis, the man responsible for building the mill, a substantial four-storey building linked to the house by a bridge. Power was provided by a huge waterwheel – 12 feet in diameter – using water pumped from the millpond on the opposite side of the road, and ran in through ditches to the mill wheel. By 1822 the water-powered factory had been converted to steam, and deeds of that year show the property consisted of quite a collection of buildings and machinery, including the 'dwelling house … workshops, factory, cottages … scribbling and carding engines, Billeys, Jennies to go with a dye furnace and blue vats', together with the steam engine.

Cloth of the finest quality

In 1834 the mill employed 95 people including children as young as nine years old and all were expected to work 11 hours – excluding the two hours allowed for meals. It produced 'Venetian cloth', a type of black wool broadcloth woven with a smooth texture and diagonal twill. It was the speciality of the mills in the Bradford-on-Avon area and that woven at Holt was reputedly the finest – 'so fine even a double width could be pulled through a wedding ring'.

An industry in decline

Towards the end of the 19th century the fortunes of the woollen industry in Wiltshire declined, a consequence of the national economic depression and also the lack of the latest technology. Ultimately the black broadcloths so familiar in Victorian England would be superseded by worsteds. As a result, the Davis family sold the heavily mortgaged property to clothier Joseph Gordon Jones from Bradford-on-Avon in 1875. He also failed to improve its fortunes and by 1885 had ceased trading.

Left empty for several years the property was purchased very cheaply by William Davis, grandson of John, who demolished the mill buildings and made some additions to the house such as the billiard room (now the Tea Room) to turn the house into a family home fit to let. However, the first person really to stamp his mark on the newly established garden was Dr, later Sir, George Hastings, who purchased The Courts in 1902

The Mart, Manvers Street, TROWBRIDGE.

To Woollen Cloth Manufacturers, Merchants, TAILORS & OTHERS.

CATALOGUE

OF AN IMPORTANT AND UNRESERVED SALE OF

WHITE SCOURED WOOLS, YARNS,

SOAP, OIL, MULE TINS AND BOBBINS,

ABOUT

3000 YARDS

OF WEST OF ENGLAND

CLOTH,

Removed from Holt Mills for convenience of Sale.

Which will be Sold by Auction,

WITHOUT RESERVE, BY

MESSRS.

BURBIDGE & GABY

By Order of Mr. J. HOWARD FOLEY, the Trustee to the Estates of Messrs. GORDON, JONES & LITTLE, of Holt Mills, near Trowbridge,

AT THE MART, MANVERS ST., TROWBRIDGE,

ON TUESDAY, JULY 28TH, 1885,

Commencing with the Wool, Yarns and Miscellaneous Effects at 12o 'clock, and the Cloth at 2 o'clock.

Catalogues may be obtained of the Auctioneers, Chippenham and Devizes, or of FOLEY & SON, The Mart, Manvers Street, Trowbridge.

J. DIPLOCK, PRINTER, TROWBRIDGE.

926/47

Opposite A view of the Lily Pond from the Dye Pool

Above Catalogue of a sale of wool, yarn and cloth removed from Holt Mills by order of the trustee of

Messrs Gordon Jones and Little, 1885

Dr George Hastings

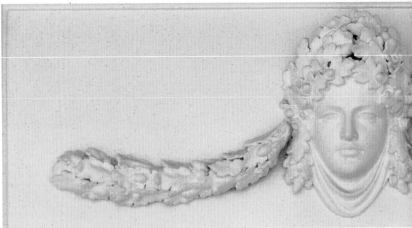

Dr George Hastings, later Sir George Hastings (1853–1943), trained at St Bartholomew's Hospital in London, and later in Brussels. He became Surgeon-Colonel to the 3rd London Rifle Volunteer Corps, physician to the Coaching, Ranelagh and Reform clubs, and subsequently the consulting surgeon to the Gas, Light and Coke Company in London. George married Alice Frith in 1878 and they had two daughters and a son. He was knighted in 1910.

Although the Hastings' tenure at The Courts was inexplicably brief, just three years, his influence on the garden has been enduring. He was responsible for much of the structure of the garden that we see today. There would have been little in the way of a garden when he bought the property, probably just a small area to the rear of the house where the Cedar Lawn is now. Most of the present garden would have been nothing more than a field. Hastings laid out the paths, planted most of the hedging, erected the garden buildings and introduced several of the various statues. Many of the garden features were copied from the gardens of the Ranelagh Club of which he was a committed member for over 40 years.

Sources of inspiration

The Ranelagh Club, not to be confused with the Ranelagh Gardens in Chelsea, was created for the enjoyment of outdoor pursuits. It was based at Barn Elms, the Georgian house in Barnes, Surrey which had been the home of the famous Kit-Cat Club in the early 18th century; it was demolished in 1954. Hastings had been influential in reviving the flagging fortunes of the club and was highly praised for his contribution to the improvements showing his interest in garden-making which he was to demonstrate at The Courts a few years later.

Above The plasterwork festoon in the Hall of the House

Left Dr George Hastings, c.1910

Opposite Stone bust of Emperor Tiberius of Rome (42BC–AD37)

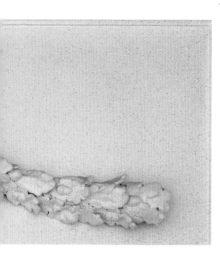

His enthusiastic involvement in the club perhaps explains why he was eager to replicate many of the ornamental features in his own garden, in particular the stone leopard.

He may also have taken inspiration from The Courts itself. The carved festoon of a face and oak leaves that adorns the pediment to Hastings' temple echoes a similar plaster one in early 18th-century style of unknown date over a door in the Hall of the House.

A coach-and-four

George Hastings was generally liked by the villagers and was a familiar sight in Holt with his 'four-in-hand and hunting horn' giving an indication of his other passion, the Coaching Club, an exclusive establishment of which he was a founder. To join, it was necessary either to own or drive a coach-and-four, and events included trips to the Ranelagh and Hurlingham clubs.

Towards the end of his life in 1939 Hastings co-wrote with Reginald Alfre an account of its history *The History of the Coaching Club 1871–1939.*

Despite all the time, money and effort that Hastings poured into The Courts, it is not known why he remained there for only three years, selling it to the Misses Trim and Barclay on 7 June 1905.

'Stately dames' The Goff family

This appears to be a fallow period in the development of the garden. Mary Trim and Helen Minnie Barclay were a striking pair, one short and tweedy, the other tall and elegant. Local chorister Jack Pafford remembered them as 'rather stately dames who kept themselves to themselves'. One was said to have been engaged to the brother of the other who unfortunately died. Little else is known about this elusive pair and their main legacy is a memorial in the churchyard to Miss Barclay's nephew who was killed in the First World War.

Although it is unlikely they neglected the garden, no evidence has come to light of any significant developments during their 15-year residence, and there is no record even of a gardener living nearby until 1921 – the year they sold up. When Major Goff purchased the property on 18 April 1921, Miss Trim and Miss Barclay had already moved to Combe Grange at nearby Monkton Combe.

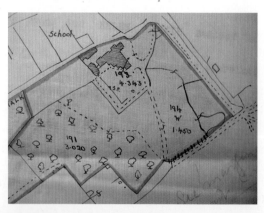

The Goffs, together with their children Tom and Moyra, moved to The Courts in 1921. Major Clarence Goff and his wife Lady Cecilie Heathcote Drummond Willoughby were married in 1896 and lived in Ireland at Carrowroe, the family estate in Roscommon where Major Goff's father had been a Member of Parliament for that constituency between 1859 and 1860. Major Goff was the great grandson of William IV (through his mistress Mrs Jordan). He had fought in both the Boer War and the First World War and was to run the Holt Home Guard during the Second World War. He was also a long-serving member of London County Council.

Lady Cecilie, daughter of the 1st Earl of Ancaster, grew up at Normanton Hall in Rutland. Her mother, a keen gardener, was influenced by Gertrude Jekyll, one of the leading lights in early 20th-century garden design. Lady Cecilie also had a scholarly interest in history. She would go on to write two books about her family: *A Woman of the Tudor Age*, a biography of her ancestor Catherine Willoughby, Duchess of Suffolk was published in 1930 and *Three Generations of a Loyal House* in 1957.

Although Carrowroe was sold in 1920, the Goffs retained certain rights, including entitlement to remove the Venetian Gates, specially made for the estate and once considered the finest in the county, and install them at The Courts where they remain at the entrance to the Arboretum.

Left The Conveyance Plan of 1921 shows the extent of The Courts when Major Goff acquired it.

Lady Cecilie Goff

Lady Cecilie had a particular flair for planting that she used to great effect at The Courts. Her husband had less influence, spending at least eight years away during the 1920s and 30s in a nursing home, leaving his wife in charge.

One of the few alterations she made was to extend the yew hedge that surrounds the formal garden, incorporating three semi-circular alcoves. Lady Cecilie was also responsible for building the large Lily Pond, and when nearby Devizes Gaol was demolished in 1927, she managed to salvage enough of its flagstones for some of the garden paths at The Courts.

Other than these few structural additions, Lady Cecilie preferred to focus on embellishing the garden with sophisticated planting schemes and choice shrubs. While little evidence exists in the form of plant lists and plans, early photographs reveal a skilled contrast of height and texture through the borders that were appreciated by Christopher Hussey. In his article for *Country Life* in 1943, he provides a valuable detailed description:

'A white and grey group around a stone urn, with Japanese anemones, the woolly leaves of mullein, *Stachys lanata*, white eschscholtzias, white alyssum and the grey foam of Artemisia and santolina, with foxgloves at the foot of the aubretia clad wall behind. The banks of the old ditch formerly supplying the mill, are thick in August with astilbes and spiraeas, their feathery plumes set off by the dark yews. The garden, indeed, is a lesson in how, without extravagant cost, advantage can be taken of the old stonework and water in which the site was so well provided.'

Above **Major Goff** (right) and Major Willoughby (left), 1929

Right **Cecilie Goff** with her dogs in the Drawing Room at The Courts, 1930s

The war years

The war was beginning to take its toll on the family and by 1943 negotiations were under way to give The Courts to the National Trust. A letter from the surveyors J.P. Sturge & Sons to the Trust in 1943 gives an insight into the amount of help the Goff's employed in the garden, as well as extolling the talents of Lady Goff herself:

'There have been employed in the past, a head gardener, a second gardener and some additional help, formerly a lad or casual helper and lately a lady who lives in the village. In addition, of course, Lady Cecilie Goff is herself an expert gardener and does a great deal …'

In a letter from Major Goff to James Lees-Milne of the National Trust in 1943, it is evident that the maintenance of the garden was a high priority and a worry. The garden he claimed:

'being a key feature of the place has always been kept up in good order and before the war I kept 3 gardeners. Now I only have 1 permanent (living in the cottage), and his working assistant who comes 2 days a week.'

The National Trust took on ownership of The Courts in 1944. Major Goff continued to live there until his death although his wife and son decided to move to London in 1946. Major Goff died in France in 1949, but his ashes were returned to Holt, and spread near the Lily Pond. His daughter Moyra became the life tenant.

During the war years the villagers in Holt collected waste paper which they sent away to

Dad's army

In 1940 Major Goff ran the Home Guard that was based at The Courts, with his head gardener, Lieutenant Stacey, by his side. The photo shows Holt Home Guard in the The Courts garden. Major Goff back row, 9th from right; Rupert Stacey back row, 10th from right

eighties was frequently seen driving her AC Cobra motor car through the village. She obviously felt a deep attachment to The Courts and initially ran the garden by herself. In 1952 she began to develop the Arboretum in the four acres that surround the formal garden. However, she struggled to retain gardening staff and was unable to maintain the garden to its former high standard.

By 1980 the National Trust decided to take a more active role, working alongside Moyra until her death in 1990. In acknowledgement of her contribution her ashes were buried around the fern-leaved beech tree in the Arboretum. The National Trust, now in sole charge of the garden, began a programme of regeneration. In the absence of plant lists or plans, the planting that exists today is largely the creation of the National Trust gardeners keen to retain the spirit of Lady Cecilie and within the original framework laid out by Hastings.

Above Lady Cecilie's newspaper collection, *The Illustrated London News*, 1941

Right Moyra Goff as a child, by Mary Lemon Waller, 1902

be made into munitions. The village won an award for collecting the largest amount of paper, as can be seen in a full-page article in *The Illustrated London News* in 1941. Lady Cecilie had a major role in this collection and a 'waste paper store' is marked on a map of The Courts which was drawn up in 1944.

Moyra Goff

Moyra Goff was a feisty and occasionally ferocious figure. She is said to have worked for the Red Cross and in an aeroplane factory during the First World War, and even in her

The Courts and the Early 20th-Century Garden

The Courts is one of the National Trust places that epitomises a key gardening approach of the early 20th century in both its structure and its planting.

Strong bones are derived from formal evergreen hedges and topiary, together with architectural features softened with relaxed and informal planting. This style can also be seen at the Trust's neighbouring Great Chalfield Manor where the garden was designed by Alfred Parsons. The Goffs knew the Fuller family who lived at Great Chalfield Manor and no doubt exchanged ideas.

Structured compartments, or rooms, of formal hedges epitomised the Edwardian and Arts and Craft garden at the beginning of the century. In 1901 a new edition of *The Formal Garden in England* by Reginald Blomfield (first published in 1892) was issued, just at the time when George Hastings was creating the structure of the garden at The Courts. Blomfield looked back to the 17th century when gardens were rigidly compartmentalised with hedges and walls creating a sense of privacy and security. In the 20th century this formality was toned down with borders of the many new herbaceous plants that were being cultivated.

A palette of colour

The Goffs were certainly influenced by Gertrude Jekyll – Lady Goff's mother is said to have consulted her on her own gardens. Jekyll was one of the most famous garden designers

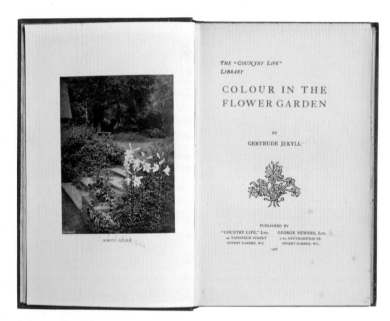

of the early 20th century although she began her career as an artist. This is reflected in the painterly way she used colour in the garden with borders of either harmonising or contrasting colours or alternatively using single colours which emphasised texture and form. Her theories were written down in several books including *Colour in the Flower Garden* and she also wrote on gardens for *Country Life*, a favourite journal of the landowning classes. Jekyll was especially

Above *Colour in the Flower Garden* by Gertrude Jekyll, 1908

Opposite top The Terrace with St Katharine's Church in the distance, 1943

Opposite below Flower border and topiary at The Courts Garden

famous for her use of foliage and texture, and the influence of this is evident in Christopher Hussey's 1943 description of The Courts, in particular 'the woolly leaves of mullein, *Stachys lanata*, white eschscholtzias, white alyssum and the grey foam of Artemisia and santolina'.

English garden style at its best

The Courts has much in common with its better-known contemporaries such as Hidcote Manor in Gloucestershire and Sissinghurst Castle in Kent – gardens where the owners rather than professionals were the creative force and all followed the same themes of formal hedges to create garden rooms, and the use of colour throughout. The particular quality of The Courts, however, lies in its industrial heritage, which lends it a unique foundation upon which the garden has evolved, and continues to evolve, to represent the best of the English garden style.

The House and the Village

The Courts has long been a prominent player in the lively Wiltshire village of Holt, originally as an employer of local people working in the woollen mill, and later during the Second World War as a base to the Home Guard.

Taking the waters

During the 18th century, Holt Spa was famous for its mineral waters which were shipped throughout the country in 'flatted' bottles. In 1730 the 'Great House' was built to accommodate visitors to the Spa; however,

Right Holt Spa token

Below The Great House at Holt Spa

decline set in with the success of the more fashionable spa at nearby Bath. In 1957 the Great House was demolished.

In the 1770s James Beaven, a woolstapler, founded a tanning business which was to become well known for its leather gloves. The company is still trading as J. & T. Beaven although there is now no on-site production. Around 1830, feather merchant Benjamin Sawtell established a mattress-making business that was to become Sleepline Beds, still trading but no longer based in Holt.

Tea with the Queen

One of the most memorable occasions was the visit by Queen Mary the Queen Mother to Holt in 1940. She visited The Courts, remaining for nearly two hours, taking tea with her hosts, the Goffs, and looking around the garden. She showed a particular interest in the relics of the former spa at Holt which were being exhibited at The Courts in aid of the National Gardens Scheme. The newspapers reported the warm welcome she received from the villagers both on her arrival and departure.

Below Queen Mary's visit to The Courts, 1940

Tour of the Garden

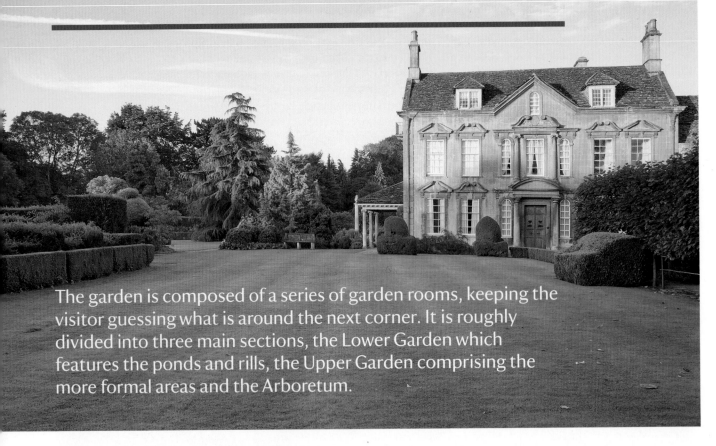

The garden is composed of a series of garden rooms, keeping the visitor guessing what is around the next corner. It is roughly divided into three main sections, the Lower Garden which features the ponds and rills, the Upper Garden comprising the more formal areas and the Arboretum.

The Lower Garden

The Entrance Lawn

The garden is approached through an iron gate and along a path flanked on either side by pleached lime trees planted in the 1980s, which replaced those originally planted in the 1950s, drawing you towards the characterful Georgian façade of the house. At the end of the path the garden opens out to reveal a large lawn surrounded by hedges and topiary – a predominant theme of the garden – softened with luxuriant herbaceous planting. This area was once the main drive but was altered by Major and Lady Goff.

The 'linenfold hedge' (imitating folded linen) that runs along the north-east boundary was probably planted by the Goffs although it is not clear whether they intended it to take on such a curious shape. The elephant's ears plant (*Bergenia cordifolia*) at the top of the rill cascade is part of the Goff's original planting.

Above The Entrance Lawn

The Pillar Lawn

The Pillar Lawn, reached by shallow steps down from the Entrance Lawn, is named after the eight stone pillars, originally linked by chains, installed by the Goffs. They were once believed to have been salvaged from the textile mill where they were used for drying the wool before weaving, although recently this theory has been rejected. Several of them had to be replaced in 2012. The Hot Beds on the south-east side originate from the early 1990s when they were planted by head gardener Troy Scott Smith. Their vibrant colours of predominantly orange, red and yellow flowers against a backdrop of purple foliage create a dramatic contrast to the green lawns and hedges. Two domes of clipped yew together with four quince trees give structure to the planting. The Fernery Pond provides a peaceful retreat in the corner, planted with cool green ferns, hostas and bamboos.

A rill that runs the length of the Pillar Lawn down to the Dye Pool is another feature that may have been influenced by the water that was diverted for the factories. The original rill was filled in during the 1920s and replaced with the ornamental one which can be seen today.

Below The Pillar Lawn

The Lily Pond

The rectangular Lily Pond, a creation of Lady Goff, appears to float amongst the surrounding plants. The still sheet of water acts as a mirror, reflecting the surrounding foliage along the Withy Walk side, and the billowy red foliage of the smoke bush (*Cotinus coggygria*), at the north-west side. A Chinese-style blue bench, copied from an original that was situated in the Cedar Lawn in 1904, contrasts with the warm colours of the smoke bush. Box topiary adds an element of structure. The pool is enhanced by Siberian iris *(Iris sibirica)* and the elegant angel's fishing rods *(Dierama pulcherrimum)*.

The raised profile of the Withy Walk runs along the eastern side of the Lily Pond. According to local rumour this is where waste from the woollen mill was deposited, resulting in very poor soil. It is probable that spoil from the pond was also piled here. In keeping with tradition the borders are planted with roses, together with yew topiaries – originally narrow obelisks on square bases – which punctuate the walk.

Opposite top The Lily Pond in 1935

Left Angel's fishing rods (*Dierama pulcherrimum*)   Below The Lily Pond

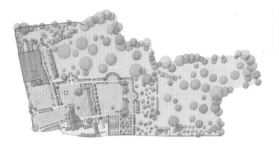

The smoke bush (*Cotinus coggygria*)
The northern side of the Lily Pond is framed by the mass of rich, purple-red foliage of several mature specimens of *Cotinus coggygria* 'Foliis Purpureis', the smoke bush. The glorious effect is magnified by its reflection in the pond. In autumn the leaves turn a rich, fiery orange-red. Its common name comes from the effect of the frothy plumes of tiny purple-pink flowers, which appear in the summer and look like puffs of smoke. The wood of the smoke bush was formerly used to produce a yellow dye known as 'young fustic', which was once used commercially in the woollen industry, a reminder of the former use of this site.

The Dye Pool

At the eastern corner of the garden, fed by water from the Lily Pond, is the Dye Pool. The name is reminiscent of the textile heritage of the site but it is unlikely to have existed at the time of the working mill. Shaded by mature trees this secluded area is dark and mysterious with naturalistic planting. The large-leaved foliage plants such as gunnera and hostas, along with ferns and bamboos create a jungle-like atmosphere. Original trees from the 1930s include the swamp cypress (*Taxodium distichum*), a rare yew (*Taxus baccata*

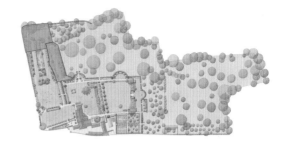

'Dovastoniana') and two birch trees (*Betula pendula* 'Youngii'), their silvery branches glowing in this shady corner. The vibrant autumn leaves of the katsura tree (*Cercidiphyllum japonicum*) smell of burnt caramel.

The Temple and Temple Borders

Flanking the long grass path that leads to George Hastings's stone Temple is a pair of generous borders, one of the highlights of the summer and autumn garden. It is planted with a considered blend of colour, texture and scale. A large holly cloud hedge can be seen above the borders and conceals the Arboretum beyond. Access can be gained to the Arboretum via a gate at the northern end of the Temple Borders. The stone-edged beds near the gates are dominated by the maidenhair tree (*Ginkgo biloba*).

Above The Temple in 1935

Below The Temple today

Pokeweed (*Phytolacca americana*) Native to North America, this plant is considered an ornamental weed. It can grow to almost three metres in height. Care must be taken when handling American pokeweed, as all parts are toxic, particularly the seeds, which can cause death to humans and livestock. Nevertheless, when correctly prepared, some parts, such as the black berries and young leaves, can be used for food or herbal medicine. The berries can also be crushed to make a red dye, which was used as ink during the American Civil War.

Opposite far left Gunnera by the Dye Pool

Opposite top The Dye Pool in 1935

Opposite below Coneflowers (*Rudbeckia*) in the Temple Border

The Upper Garden

The Cedar Lawn

The Cedar Lawn is the pivotal point in the garden through which most visitors will pass. Many elements of Sir George Hastings' garden can be seen here, including the column with bust on top and the stone orb in the paved square. The stone leopard on the Terrace steps is a copy of one from the Ranelagh Club. A small courtyard garden next to the Conservatory is shaded by an old yew tree, a possible survivor from the mill days. A water feature in the form of a basin and water spout flows into a small pond planted with iris and dryopteris.

Hastings also laid out the yew hedge but semicircular niches were added at a later date by the Goffs. Established cedar and mulberry trees are depicted in early photographs and were probably planted before Sir George Hastings moved here. Although both trees have since died, they have been replaced to ensure a degree of continuity.

The beautiful Venetian Gates seem rather grand for this English country garden; the Goffs had them specially made for their estate in Ireland around 1912. When they moved to The Courts they brought the gates with them. Today they make a fine entrance to the Arboretum, draped with the blue bell-like flowers of *Clematis alpina* 'Frances Rivis'. The Orb Beds at the eastern end were originally designed as a formal centrepiece and have recently been replanted.

Opposite **Topiary**

Left **A stone column with bust on the Cedar Lawn**

Left below **The stone leopard on the Terrace**

Below right *Clematis alpina* **'Frances Rivis' growing over the Venetian Gates**

Below **Architect's drawing of the Venetian Gates**

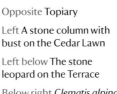

Giant feather grass *(Stipa gigantea)*
With their subtle hues and fragile elegance, catching the light and rippling in the breeze, grasses add an ethereal dynamic to the borders. This can be clearly seen with the massed planting of *Stipa gigantea* in the Golden Yew Walk beside the Cedar Lawn. The grasses flower briefly in late May and June, but the large, feathery seed heads carry on the show all the way through the winter, hinting at sunlight, even on dull days and providing a golden accent against the dark evergreen backdrop of the yew hedge behind.

The Terrace

Dividing the Main Lawn from the Cedar Lawn are the Terrace Beds. The raised Terrace, designed by Lady Goff, gives some variety to the otherwise flat terrain of the garden and offers raised views over either side of the garden. Eight metal poles of old pipework found in the gardens in the 1920s and 30s were recycled to create a garden feature. Today they support vines of contrasting colour – the crimson glory vine (*Vitis coignetiae*), and the common grape vine (*Vitis vinifera*). Tall ornamental grasses such as African feather grass (*Pennisetum macrourum*) and silver pampas grass (*Cortaderia selloana*) have since been added to emphasise the vertical accents.

The curious yews planted in the 1920s, are known as 'the Dancing Bears'.

Salsify (*Tragopogon porrifolius*) From June to September the Cedar Lawn, Terrace and Queen Elizabeth Bed are dotted with the long, strappy leaves and pinky-purple daisy flowers of the self-sown *Tragopogon porrifolius*. This is salsify, or the 'vegetable oyster', which can be grown for its roots (a little like parsnip) and dug up at the end of its first year. The wonderful show of flowers it produces during its second year is followed by a display of striking golden seed heads, reminiscent of dandelion clocks.

The Yew Walk

The Yew Walk encompasses a winding stone path edged by giant Irish yews (*Taxus baccata* 'Fastigiata') and a mixed border of mainly herbaceous perennials. These include yarrow (*Achillea filipendulina* 'Cloth of Gold'), Crocosmia 'Lucifer' and globe thistle (*Echinops bannaticus*).

The Main Lawn

The Main Lawn is a grand sweep of grass surrounded by diverse borders and topiary, the centre stage of the whole garden. A row of giant Irish yews (*Taxus baccata* 'Fastigiata'), originally designed as regimented pillars to complement the formality of the Main Lawn, has over the years taken on a more organic, almost drunken appearance, now adding a light-hearted contrast. The yew hedge to the south-east side of the lawn is indented with a semicircular alcove sheltering a pair of green benches. Around the corner to the western side of the Main Lawn are the Yellow and Blue Borders with the contrasting colours of the Russian sage (*Perovskia atriplicifolia* 'Blue Spire') and the pale yellow *Achillea* 'Moonshine'. A small flight of steps leads to the Sundial Lawn,

Above The Yellow and Blue Borders on the Main Lawn

Below The Sundial Lawn in the mid-1930s

Woodland crocus
(*Crocus tommasinianus*)
Affectionately known as 'Tommies', these are the earliest flowering crocuses and one of the highlights of the garden in early spring. They can be naturalised in grass and, once settled, are prolific self-seeders. The resulting carpet of flowers, in subtle shades ranging from silvery lilac to rosy purple is spellbinding, especially when the sun shines and their petals open wide. They also provide a welcome early source of food for bees.

Left The Kitchen Garden

Below right The water spout

Below right The apple *allée* in autumn

trees, an apple *allée*, clipped box hedging and regimented rows of vegetables. Herbs are grown underneath the apple cordons. Today the vegetable garden is managed organically and planted with heritage varieties where appropriate. It is also used to illustrate kitchen-gardening techniques.

The Orchard

Once the Goffs' tennis court, the Orchard is now a transitional space between the formal garden and the informal Arboretum and is bordered by both old and new pear espaliers and cloud box hedging. It is home to a collection of heritage apple varieties.

enclosed within another alcove in the hedge, a perfect place to sit and absorb the garden. Further along, on the boundary border with the Kitchen Garden, is the Crocus Bed, heralding springtime with a sea of pale blue *Crocus tommasinianus*. The path to the north of the Main Lawn is edged with a fine selection of peonies, including 'Sarah Bernhardt', 'Shirley Temple', 'Bowl of Beauty' and 'Charles' White'.

The Sunken Garden

Entirely enclosed by a beech hedge this hidden garden was rebuilt in 2003 with stone-walled raised beds. Its design is ongoing.

The Kitchen Garden

The layout of the original kitchen garden was lost when it was grassed over following years of neglect, although a few apple trees have survived. The present Kitchen Garden is situated in the same position but does not extend as far. Despite being a relatively recent addition, it feels very traditional, having a formal design which incorporates trained fruit

The Arboretum

Left The Lower Arboretum

The Arboretum, extending to four acres, provides a relaxed contrast to the formal gardens. Developed in 1953 by Moyra Goff, many of the trees have now reached full maturity. The majority are broad-leaved deciduous species conveying the gentle character of an English woodland. A spectacular fern-leaved beech (*Fagus sylvatica* var. *heterophylla* 'Aspleniifolia') takes centre stage but other trees to look out for include sweet gum (*Liquidamber styraciflua*) with its vibrant autumn colour, the Indian bean tree (*Catalpa bignonioides*), and the tulip tree (*Liriodendron tulipifera*). In the spring the ground is carpeted with scillas, varieties of narcissus and snake's head fritillaries (*Fritillaria meleagris*). In 1995 Elizabeth Sargeant, a great supporter of the garden, donated 150,000 Siberian squill bulbs (*Scilla siberica*) which were planted in the Arboretum to commemorate the National Trust's Centenary. Each bulb represented ten members of the National Trust at that date.

The Wildlife Garden

This area of the garden was created in 2005 by the children of Holt Primary School under the stewardship of the National Trust's Guardianship Scheme and has continued to develop ever since. As well as being used for outdoor learning opportunities, it is also a secret area where children of all ages can experience a very different part of The Courts, hidden away from the rest of the garden.

The dove tree (*Davidia involucrata*)

Davidia involucrata was first recorded in 1886 by Père David, a French missionary and botanist, working in Peking. In 1899, plant hunter Ernest Wilson arrived in China specifically to collect the seed of the tree, with the express instruction from his employer, Veitch Nursery, not to waste time, energy or money on anything else. He first visited another plant hunter, Augustine Henry, who supplied him with a sketch map that covered many hundreds of square miles marked with the rough location of the one dove tree he had seen some 12 years earlier. It took Wilson months of trekking to pinpoint the area – and when he did, he discovered only the stump of a tree, next to a newly built timber house … It took him several months more searching before he found another!

Gardeners with a Vision

The Courts represents the talents not only of the owners but also its gardeners.

Below Rupert Stacey with his gardening team, around 1940.

An 'irreplaceable loss'

When Major and Lady Goff moved here in 1921 a Mr Harris is recorded as living in Court Cottage, and it is likely he was responsible for the maintenance of the garden although little is known about his involvement. However, by 1937 Rupert Stacey was employed as head gardener and, while Lady Cecilie was undoubtedly the driving force in the garden, Stacey was acknowledged for his valuable contribution. A member of the Holt Home Guard, he was known locally as 'Lieutenant Stacey'. The relationship between the Goffs and their head gardener was undoubtedly a good one, and several photographs of Stacey and his family were taken in the garden.

Sadly in 1944, a day after the handover to the Trust, Stacey died unexpectedly of a heart attack at the age of 59. Major Goff's distress is obvious in his letter to Lees-Milne, the secretary of the Country Houses Committee of the National Trust: 'We have a sad tragedy here, my gardener died suddenly last Friday night, his loss is irreplaceable. It is almost impossible to find an equally good one, or one at all. I fear I must let the garden RIP.'

The loss was felt on a personal level as the inscription on their floral tribute testified 'In affectionate memory of a true friend'.

A man for all seasons

Between 1944 and 1946 Major Goff employed Col. Harry Thompson Russell as his head gardener. A colonel who fought in the Boer War,

he went on to write entertaining phrase books such as *Brighter French: Colloquial & Idiomatic, for Bright Young People (who already know some)*. He lived in the gardener's cottage at The Courts where his wife, Marion, also helped in the garden.

For the next 40 years a succession of head gardeners oversaw the maintenance of The Courts, but there was little development. Ralph Gibbon was the longest serving, taking up his post in 1959 and staying until 1979.

Andrew Humphris was employed as head gardener at The Courts during the final years of Moyra Goff's life. When she died in 1990, the National Trust was for the first time in sole control of the garden. Andrew worked at The Courts for ten years before becoming the Trust's head gardener at Biddulph Garden.

Above Harry Thompson Russell

Bringing the past into the future

It was not until 1997 that a young gardener, trained at Sissinghurst Castle and with an understanding of 20th-century gardens, was given the responsibility of breathing new life into The Courts. Troy Scott Smith's vision was to restore the garden to its original vibrancy. He made improvements and additions which allowed the garden to evolve while still retaining the spirit of its former incumbents. Beds around the house were enlarged and the overgrown yew hedges were pruned back to reveal the original structure of the garden, and the borders were enhanced with colour-themed perennials. Perhaps his most obvious contribution was the re-creation of the Kitchen Garden and Orchard which has since become one of the garden's most popular areas.

A 'fantastic plantswoman'

Cat Saunders, an archaeologist by training, succeeded Troy Scott Smith as head gardener in 2005; she relished the challenge of its intensity of planting and its high horticultural standards. She continued to develop the atmosphere of the garden and researched the history of the garden and house. Graham Heard, general manager at The Courts, said: 'Cat was a fantastic plantswoman who got really stuck into the planning and care of the borders and spent every minute she could in the garden with sleeves rolled up, head down and at one with the soil.'

She also dealt with the largest aesthetic change in recent times – the reduction of the overpowering lime trees along Withy Walk – by re-pollarding them back to their traditional size, letting in light to open up this whole side of the garden.

A lasting legacy

In 2010 Paul Alexander took over as head gardener. His vision for the garden is to build on the legacy of his predecessors, focusing on its long-term potential by redeveloping parts of the garden that have become over-mature, maintaining the sharp profile of the topiary and hedges, and introducing water collection and irrigation systems.

The individual character of The Courts rather than its academic significance has enabled the garden to evolve while maintaining the spirit of the place. Careful conservation of precious features, high horticultural standards and a respect for the natural environment will ensure the continued development of the garden for both the enjoyment of the local community and the interest of garden enthusiasts alike.

Top Troy Scott Smith

Above Cat Saunders

Right Paul Alexander at work in The Courts Garden